Echoes of Retrospection

Monyet`

Order this book online at www.trafford.com
or email orders@trafford.com

Most Trafford titles are also available at major online book retailers.

Note for Librarians: A cataloguing record for this book is available from Library
and Archives Canada at www.collectionscanada.ca/amicus/index-e.html

Printed in Victoria, BC, Canada.

ISBN: 978-1-4269-1469-0 (sc)

Library of Congress Control Number: 2009932246

*We at Trafford believe that it is the responsibility of us all, as both individuals
and corporations, to make choices that are environmentally and socially sound.
You, in turn, are supporting this responsible conduct each time you purchase
a Trafford book, or make use of our publishing services. To find out how you
are helping, please visit www.trafford.com/responsiblepublishing.html*

*Our mission is to efficiently provide the world's finest, most comprehensive book publishing
service, enabling every author to experience success. To find out how to publish your
book, your way, and have it available worldwide, visit us online at www.trafford.com*

Trafford rev. 08/14/09

Trafford
PUBLISHING® www.trafford.com

North America & international
toll-free: 1 888 232 4444 (USA & Canada)
phone: 250 383 6864 ♦ fax: 250 383 6804 ♦ email: info@trafford.com

To my Lord and Savior Jesus Christ for always being faithful even when I am not. There are no words that adequately express my love for you, so my greatest expression is to live a life most pleasing to you!

To my mother, Cynthia C. Hundley-Green, words cannot begin to express all that you mean to me. You are an extraordinary and phenomenal woman to say the least and in time I will tell your story and it will touch the world...because love transcends all things. I love you over and over again and again some more. You have been my example and prayer warrior. I am in awe of where the Lord is taking you as you reach the next level in Him.

To my grandfather, the late Clarence Green, Sr. (Pop-pop), when I was a child you were the greatest grandfather a little girl could ever have. I love you just the same.

Love is sacrificial and at times painful,
yet more than just an emotion.

Table of Contents

The Master and His Plan

To my mother, for your outstanding accomplishments in life.

**'The monetary value of an education is irrelevant to the
experience, but persevering and esteeming one's self in
the face of injustice; with dignity and poise is the greatest
accomplishment known to man.'-Monyet**

Your legacy began nearly thirty years ago
When you gave birth to me,
-neither you nor I knew the Plan of God, but yet you pressed ahead
setting the blueprint for what would ultimately become my road
map and compass for life,
But in the course of my journey you equipped me with the Master
of this Plan
The man who would become my shield and buckler, provider,
comforter, and father,
In Him lied my strength, wisdom, and knowledge
In Him lied my life and in Him lied the reason for my being,
And in you He ignited the strength to raise not only me, but also
three more which came after me
During his ignition of strength in you
He began to sculpt you and prepare you for the trials that lied
ahead
For He knew His voice you'd heed and His instructions you'd
follow
For in Him lied your source for living because in Him there is life
and without Him there is none.

He knew you'd be faithful and obedient

He knew you could handle what He was about to entrust in you

As you heeded His voice, obeyed His instructions, the test of your faith in Him began

Through the pain, hurt, disappointment, anger, and during the revelation of His word coming to pass,

You knew the Master of the Plan was in control,

You knew He would keep you, through the pain, hurt and many many weary days,

You knew He'd keep you,

Not knowing how or when, you knew He'd show up even if it was no more than for His namesake,

You relied solely on the Master-

Steadfast, unmovable, and faithful

It was a test of your faith and could you stand?

The question was not for the Master to answer

-for He knew it before He gave it to you

It was a refining process for you, a metamorphic phase because indeed-

You needed to know what you are and who you are,

You are what He said you are,

An over comer, triumphant, victorious, a conqueror-but not just a conqueror, more than a conqueror

A virtuous woman, who has the heart of the Master, the favor of His heart, The illumination of His love, and the strength and soul of His spirit and ways-

Your legacy I say began with me, but it began many years before me, before you, it began in the mind of the Master

He prepared and sculpted you and through Him you equipped me
Your legacy is that of faith, triumphs, and your unwavering trust
ad belief that He created a place where you'd stand before men in a
large room,
Holding the hardcopy of His master plan,
More than a testimony, but a witness knowing the Master for
whom He is
And what He has done!

The End Times

It's a sad day when our youth have lost their innocence,
When our young black minds are being destroyed by instant
gratification,
The lust of the eye is more futile than the hands that use to till the
land in the days of old,
It's a sad day when our youth are disgruntled and tormented by
societal woes that have plagued a culture for decades and yet seeps
into their pores
And extracts through the eyes of the little minds of children who
believe they live in a defeated nation without reprise
It's a sad day when our playgrounds are screenplays broadcast
throughout the nightly news
As a preview of an uneventful massacre ending in bloodshed and
the death of young boys not barely old enough to read
It's a sad day when you read the newspaper of a young girl age 5,
raped and killed, whose body was found slain in a ditch covered in
debris and garbage just five blocks from her home,
It's a sad day when babies are being disposed instead of being born
Their dreams merely dots to an "I" and their heartbeats just a sign
of life somehow suffocated by a woman who could care less
It's a sad day when our children aren't children at all anymore,
When they are running the homes they are to be raised in and
making decisions, while raising their parents and caring for their
siblings,
We have the young nurturing the younger, as the old nurture their
addictions, egos and emotions, neglecting their responsibilities

and losing their souls in the process, by indulging in the temporal extremities of this world.

It's a say day when you see the plight of the world's failures and tragedies being exploited as a wondrous extravaganza, when good deeds are overlooked and despised instead of being embraced as sign of progress in stride and consciousness of pride and good will.

It's a sad day when the currency of exchange in this country has lost its value and the powers that be debate over whether "IN GOD WE TRUST" ought to be replaced by some non-entity who leads a revolt against the nation they knew nothing about.

IT is sad when we have forgotten that GOD is why we exist not some scientific notion or big bang theory by far, and if we look at the sign of the times,

We are indeed living in the end times, which we will soon have to give an account for all the immoral sentiments that have taken place and then and only then will the world see,

-that judgment day is at hand

That GOD himself is the womb of time that predicates the beginning and the end, which cannot be changed, reversed nor destroyed.

Be Strong

I saw you today and you were blatantly fed up
>Fed up with the situation you are in

You felt closed in and suffocated
>No where to go, no where to run

Tired of the drama, false hopes, and empty promises
>You felt like a caged bird wanting to be freed

I saw you wanting to throw up your hands and give up
>You were warring against your will to maintain and your
>desire to do you

You're perplexed and exhausted
>You are a man constantly going through changes

Some say necessary but others say not so necessary
>Remember all things work together for your good,

Trials refine you and contribute to the betterment of your growth---
>Just don't give up.

It is important that you hang in there...
>Frustration will only enable you to do, say, and become the
>very thing you despise.

I know this is easier said than done but,
>The object of trials is elevation, both naturally and spiritually

I encourage you, care for you, and love you, but I will not pacify you
>This is the time for you to become stronger to get yourself
>together,

For the trying of your faith worketh patience or have you forgotten?
>This is not the time for you to give in to your emotions,

This is the time for you to stand strong and firm,

Knowing that this too shall pass.

Why falter? When you are a warrior, a soldier not prone, bred, or taught failure.

In case you have forgotten all things are subject to change, Your inert ability is strength,

So by all means, don't give up.

Be strong, be valiant, and walk in expectation knowing your change is coming.

Hold fast and stand assured of your deliverance.

Sisters

Sisters, we are mocha, amaretto, hazelnut, honey, coal
complexioned, and tawny brown
We are slim, big boned, hippy, busty, voluptuous, and shapely
We are the universal givers of life,
We are conscious motivators, who create opportunities; we enhance
the lives we mold,
We are power and refuge, we create and set standards, and in the
workplace, we shatter barriers,
We thread our existence in society and proclaim our place in a
sector, whose societal infrastructure began with man,
We are the forerunners for our children and the strength behind our
men,
We are the echoes of our mothers who birthed not only life but, our
dreams
We endure pain, induce joy, and conceive life
Sisters we are the nucleus of our communities,
And wealth lies within our souls,
We are protective, opinionated doers, who love hard; we give our
all, and strive beyond what we see,
Our vision enables us to obtain the intangible for we are believers of
the impossible,
We are divinely appointed to be influential in words, deeds, and
actions of men and the things we have sown in them, so although
we are seen but not always heard;
Yet we are strongly felt as we ignite the thoughts of our men

Sisters we are indeed the silent voices who are felt among the masses of those who fail to acknowledge the origins of their existence.

So for the life of me, I can not begin to internalize the realities of disparate treatment we experience from time to time

When we are fruitful and multiplexed, and we are the essence that defines class.

I am your strength and you are mine.

We are sisters.

In Memory

I remember you,
-never thought I would have to rely on memories of you, of us, of
how much you meant to me,
About how our friendship evolved,
About how time would somehow force me to accept the many
truths of who we were,
I remember you.
I remember you,
Your cool, calm, collected disposition, your unspoken words of
caring for me,
-your unwavering commitment to me when I needed you the most,
Usually during those unexpected moments, when you were off
doing your thang,
Your forthright stance in loving me even when I was difficult at
times,
-you accepted me for me, and yes I remember you.
I remember your smile, your laughter, the joy in your voice, the
sincerity of your manhood, you were real at all times, and
For that I remember you.
I remember those phone calls at two and three in the morning,
Our early morning breakfast at the diner,
Our long talks about your dreams, your life, and the love for your
children,
We were connected; we had years of friendship invested from
childhood through college.
It's that I remember, when I remember you.

I remember calling you, paging you, trying to get in touch with you,
And no answer, it was unlike you to not return my calls,
To not answer my pages, to not get back in touch with me,
It was highly unusual
Then out of the blue, I get a phone call and was told you had passed.
-that your life had come to an abrupt end.
The details I was given put me in a state of numbness, I was
devastated, in denial, my mind went into a series of illusions and
before I knew it my heart fell as did the tears.
There I sat drenched in a whirlwind of indescribable tears full of
emotions and despair.
You were my best friend, a man I loved more than I cared to express
at times,
You were my confidant, my laughter and joy; you were my thrill
and high all in one.
You were serious about life, about love, you were precise and exact.
I never had to wonder about you but-
-at that moment I wondered and questioned how I would fill my
life without you.
Who would I talk to?
Who would love me as you did?
Who would accept me so willingly as you had and
Who would be my best friend?
Who could ever compare to you?
I remember you, I remember you like it was yesterday,
I remember you today, and I'll remember you tomorrow
It seems the memories haven't faded
I remember you and still feel the love I felt when you were here,

When you filled the moments of my life
I'll remember as your love lingers throughout my mind and within
my heart,
I will forever remember you, as the man who birthed and redefined
friendship and love for a woman like me.

Dedicated to Peanut.

Reluctance

She was loving him,
Exemplifying all the love she had to give in thoughts and deeds, yet
She refused to consummate the relationship,
The uncertainty of love in return enabled her to maintain and refrain
From giving him all she had to give-
Including the rights and privileges of experiencing the woman
within,
He was loving her
In actions and deeds a man of very few words,
He wanted to show her love
He wanted her to experience him and all he had to give
He was reluctant to give her the most important part of him
His heart.
He was loving her, but the possibility of another unfulfilled
relationship stayed his hand,
He maintained and refrained from giving her his heart,
They loved one another,
He her
Her him
Yet the two lacked the essence of it all…communication and
oneness;
And an exclusive session entailing a meeting of the minds, to define
The exact likeness of the love held between them both.
A love clouded by fear and reluctance.

New Love

I thought of you today,

I missed you today,

I needed you today,

I love you more today than perhaps I did yesterday

I thought of your laughter----the glimmer in your eyes

I imagined you and me ecstatically loving one another, caressing one another, holding one another.

I missed you today,

That early morning wake up call

The excitement in your voice

The love that exuberates through your heart

I needed you today,

I needed to know you were beside me,

That you were mine, and

Together we were not just emotionally attached but physically as well

I loved you today, perhaps more than I did yesterday or the day before

It's not that I loved you any less those days

It's just that today my love seems to overpower all the emotions of effectual stimulation from my heart to my mind

It's just that today I would invoke love on you and you would know that today,

I really love you perhaps more than I did yesterday, not that yesterday you didn't know I loved you but---

Today is a new day, birthed by a new fragrance of love which infuses a new picture of our love,

That genuinely gives you a little something-something extra for the love I feel today,

It's just that today you would feel love as if it was love for the very first time all over again,

Today you would feel the anxiousness of love's feelings----you would

Know the excitement of love's sincerity,

You would endorse love as a priceless monument holding newly discovered history in the making

I thought of you today

I missed you today

I needed you today

I love you today, perhaps more than I did yesterday, but tomorrow will be the beginning of love all over again.

Oneness

She loves him; he is an extension of her greatness, which
compliments her essence
He ignites passion and provokes her to dream
She is the fire that thrusts high to surpass any obstacle that may
seem to hinder his progress,
Together they are a force, united by common oneness, perilous times
and indescribable experiences that only they know and understand,

He loves her, he feels her, he breathes her, and he sleeps her,
He is in love with her
And love is what they share.

She is enamored by him; she is his strength, his resource in life,
She sustains him, encourages him, loves him, needs him, is
mesmerized by him,
She is in love with him and love is what they share.

She hinges on the hope of the everlasting,
She enjoys him
She welcomes the challenges they encounter,
She is wise
She is uplifting and soothing to him
If he could express her in one word it would be phenomenal.
If he could cite her beauty it would be distinctive
If he could reveal her heart it would be protected
If he could have one wish

It would be to love her from beginning to end and all over again,
For she is desirable and rare
To him, she is love and love is what they share.
He is man over matter,
He is strong, compassionate, and determined
He is real and exact
He loves in all sectors relating to her,
She is loving in all matters that are pleasing to him,
They are in love and love is what they share.

You Wish

We've been together for nearly two years
Two long memorable, loving yet pain filled years
I grew to trust you, grew to love you
It was a learning process for real, cause I'm not the one to love easily
yet alone quickly,
So every bit of love you got,
Believe you me it was all true
Now that you feel the love has faded,
Lost its luster, spark and passion,
Do me a favor and do you.
Cause as you ought to know
This here woman is not in the business of trying to keep a man who
doesn't wan to be kept
No hold bars, just step out, go, keep it real and do you
It was what it was, no more no less
Our time has come to an end and what?
I have no regrets, won't forget what we shared, but I'd be darned if I
get you to stay
Stay?
Nah, I don't even want you to
You thought I'd be hurt?
You look almost disappointed as if you wish you could take back
what you said.
You want out so be it.

You see I'm just not in the business of trying to keep a man who doesn't want to be kept.
From the expression on your face, I get the impression you want me to ask you to stay,
You want me to ask for us to work things out, as if this is a mistake
I am not that one, even though you wish I was!

Trust is Hard

Trust is hard to come by
Hard, too hard
You can say this and that but-
It doesn't mean a thing
You can do what you say the majority of the time
But still it doesn't mean a thing
Why?
Trust is hard to come by, just because you appear to say what you mean and do what you say
Doesn't mean your inner being is driving you to say what you say or do what you do
Nah, I'm afraid not
If that's all I have to go on that alone is not enough for me to put my trust in you
You see call me the mistress of ceremonies,
I have regulated the game of quest and conquer,
I've said things and done things consistently, precisely as I've spoken them, but truth is
It didn't mean a thing
It was a matter of longevity
How long could I do what I was doing and have the next man believe me as he had me believe him,
Believe my love was real and ultimately trust me
I had been lied to more times than I can remember so I studied the game and mastered it,
Mastered it so well if ever I had to I could run game,

Yes game, it's usually a man's world, but I assure you I'm a rare breed,
A high profile woman with more game that the normal game runner is liable to get sidetracked by my quick tongue and nonchalant attitude, ghettofied antics and subtle tactics, just too raw and too intelligent for it to be male dominated,
So don't think I trust you because it ain't even on the books, not even part of the game.
Yes, trust is hard to come by,
Hard too hard,
So I advise you never think for one minute that I trust you,
As far as I'm concerned you're still suspect.

Reality

You're there and I'm here
Now that's reality
I sit and ponder what could be but the bottom line is I only wish.
There are so many things I'd like to share with you, but would you
understand?
Could you understand enough to appreciate me for the woman I am?
I only wish you could.
Every thing's a new, I mean everything, but----am I to wait for the
right time to reveal my feelings?
Time is definitely a factor, but am I to wait for time or should I step
out on the real?
The real is, you're there and I'm here
I'm talking about reality,
You're not up close and personal, but it ain't nothing, because in the
morning I think of you
Mid day my thoughts are of you and by late day,
I'm consumed by the whole notion of you, then again, that's my
reality
For some strange unexplained reason
I can think of no one but you
Perhaps I've created an image of you that's far from who you
actually are,
I've tried to let go,
I want to let go, but in all honesty
I can never seem to really let you go
That's the reality I face everyday

I'm a good woman, bittersweet all in the same,

Committed to a bad boy by name,

Converted himself and changed his name, slick, sly hardcore, yet sensual,

I seem to stick with him no matter what he pulls,

On the flip side of things, it's a one sided ordeal,

Negotiations ceased way back when,

His feelings for me ended before mine began,

That's reality.

So why do I continue as if everything is everything, when it isn't?

The more time passes, the more I've gotten away from reality

But the reality is you're there and I'm here----

No commitments, no promises, no future plans, just words of endearment to ease your wounded ego.

Reality is the implied notion that you have love for the moment,

But words of love any man can utter from a distance…

Now if that isn't reality.

When

When will I stop loving him?

When will I be able to forget these feelings?

When I hear the song he use to sing as he sat engulfed in me?

When will I not long to have him next to me, holding me, making me feel safe and secure?

When will I be able to think of him and not have the course of my day interrupted?

When will I be able to talk about him without feeling saddened by the separation of us?

When will I be able to see him and not feel immense displeasure and the emotional urgency to run away and cry out of mere discontentment?

When will these feelings pass?

When will I stop loving him?

When will I have an emotional change of heart and fall out of love with him?

Just tell me when?

I've been toiling over loving him, in disbelief, it can't be over

How did it get to this point, where it's his love I miss and long for?

How did I allow myself to get so emotionally attached?

Love, the love we shared.

The love I once knew,

When?

Yes, when will it fade like rain on a hot day, after the sun begins to shine?

Will I be able to get over him and not feel the sudden impact of ruptured dreams, senseless love, and emotional turmoil of what if's and other potential improbabilities because it's over?
All I need is a sense of closure but when?

A Far Off

Loves a far off
I don't feel what you feel
As a matter of fact,
I'm not sure you know what it is you feel,
But I can assure you it's not love
You see love is a choice
Either it is or it isn't
All I know is I don't choose to love you
Why?
Simple.
If I were to choose to love you
I would be subjecting myself to the illegitimate consignments of a
man
Who doesn't know how to love monogamously
He thrives off of polygamy, regimentation, and aggression
In other words,
It'll be all about you and only you
And in essence I'd merely be a shadowed image for you to toy with
whenever you get ready
You'd control, regulate, and define what it is
I should be and when I'm to be it
I'd have to move, breathe, and speak at your tentative command
and only then
So you see, I could never choose to love you because I would never
allow your feelings of love to stagnate and minimize me to fit into
your own dismal fallacy of how love should be

Choosing to love you would only give you the impression
I surrendered my free will and became totally subservient to you
Something you should know would never go down because I'm too
Outspoken and well versed for a man like you and---
My ability to out talk you would only frustrate you and have you
feeling nothing but contempt towards me,
So I'm telling you
Loves a far off----so far it can't be seen and it sure can't be felt
Love is a choice,
Either it is or it isn't
So umm, think about it.
Now tell me, it really isn't love after all, now is it?

Without You

What would I do without you?
I'm accustomed to the reality of loving you,
I'm at a stance where I can't see myself letting you go
For once this is love worth fighting for
Now, I know what I have to do to make this relationship work.
It has taken me what seems like forever to accept the fact you won't
let me go either
I was caught up in the tragedies of past loves, false hopes, and
ridiculous illusions of what I was led to believe and
I vowed the next time I wouldn't trust so easily,
I wouldn't believe so hastily, and I wouldn't accept so willfully, but I
would be cautious, assured and absolutely certain that the love was
right.
It's not that I think I'm unworthy of being loved, or that
I string up or premeditate drama to keep you upset and frustrated
But sometimes I over analyze things that has happened between us
and then the questions begin,
Doubts set in, and before you know it I'm interrogating you as if
you betrayed me
We always end up going through the motions of getting re-
acquainted, setting the record straight, and putting everything out
on the table, hoping-
It will be the last time we'll have to go through something that was
thought to be resolved a long time ago
It's hard for me to believe and accept the fact you love me,
Why wouldn't you?

After all you know what you have in me---no questions asked and no doubts lingering

Your confidence lies in me because you know love won't let me leave you, do you wrong, or even conjure up a thought to set you outside the confines of my heart.

So what you need to understand is I had no intentions on falling in love with you,

I had no idea this time around I wouldn't be able to remove my emotions so easily or that my heart would fight me strongly

The thought of loving you for a lifetime has me nervous and afraid. Why?

This time I don't know what I would do without you, if-

Suddenly you decided you didn't want this relationship anymore,

The thought of investing so much time, for it to end has me trippin'

Cause it would be hard for me to stop loving you

It would be just as difficult for me to pick up and love again

I wasn't looking for love, I didn't seek you out

Loving you was unexpected and took some time,

Even then I was afraid to tell you, I tried to fight it, but the more I saw you, the clearer it became

Soon time would prove my feelings to be real.

You need to know for me you are everything I want and need

You are the man, I need to be sure this is where you want to be

It's not a matter of explaining yourself to me,

It's you having the heart to convey and express the love you have for me

It's not what you say, most times, to convince me everything's going to be all right

It comes down to how well you handle me and how things will work out,

The thought of loving you is enough to have any woman in love trippin' at the most unexpected times,

It's not my intention to have you repeat yourself over and over again,

I don't know if I could ever stop loving you

I don't know what I would do without you,

I just don't know and don't want to ever know because I intend for us to be together for as long as whenever

So when you say you're not giving up on our relationship,

I hope you stay that way

I hope you continue to feel we have something worth saving.

I hope you continue to care enough to put up with my over analytical, hardheaded, stubborn, got to be right, know-it-all, near perfect, didn't hear it right the first time, self that seems to eat at you whenever you feel like I'm forcing you to explain yourself when you don't feel like you should.

I hope you continue to love me even when we agree to disagree, and argue to make up because if you truly ever stopped loving me,

I just don't know what I would do without you.

Retired Player

You had many women, all shades, shapes and sizes
You had a different woman to suit your moods on a day-to-day basis
But still couldn't commit
Every time I turned around someone was having your baby,
Another child born, another woman torn, another life ruined yet
you kept on moving,
You actually believed you loved them all.
In and out of lives,
You came to and fro not really knowing what you wanted.
You claimed you needed no one, and
That you did what you did because you could
After all you were the man
Every woman wanted to be touched and sprinkled by your smooth,
seduction, suave and sensual flow of uprising motions,
Deemed the master of ceremonies
You ran more lives,
Told more lies than the average man did in year's time
A walking sperm bank, a baby manufacturer, the joker's wild
and daddy to more than just one woman's child
Then out of the blue something began to happen
You met a woman who cared not to entertain your slick words,
cunning schemes, and blatant lies
For once in your life, you met a strong independent woman with
more game than you ever dreamed imaginable.
She had you perplexed and tongue stutter stung by her exactness
and confidence

You couldn't hit and run because you didn't get that far

Steady trying to chip away at her

You thought you could break her down, capture her, and put her in a state of mere oblivion,

Yet the more you tried the more difficult it became,

This woman was like no other, she was untouchable, unmovable, too arrogant, too confident, all wrong too right, stringy with her goodies, too right but all wrong for you-

No night became the right night; you were in a maze that left you in a corner wondering which way do you go? How will you flow? When will she give in?

A day became a week, a week became two weeks, two weeks became a month, a month soon became three months and three months became a year; and still nothing had changed.

You became frustrated, uneasy, dissatisfied, disappointed with your weak tactics and sorry schemes

What shook you up was the fact you felt something you hadn't felt with no other woman before

Every no became a why and mere silence left you feeling foul

A player's player, you lost the feel of the game

How could the master of ceremonies call it quits, the joker's wild of more than one woman's child

Now an ex-freelance sperm donor just folded

Left to yourself, you soon realized the first time in your life you actually felt love

But how could you convince this rare and exact woman you truly loved her

Everywhere you turned it seemed as if everyone wanted her

Your homeboy, the brother next door, your brother's boy
Now it's not about the score, it's about winning at love
It's about gaining a partner for life,
It's do or die; it's a matter of sacrifice
The originator of the game
The player of all-star players soon became a retired player, an
inspired brother set out to gain love.

Expired

I know everything's for the moment
You're buying time slowly
As the clock winds down so do you only because I was the one who
held us together
If ever I stopped it would be the end of us
You don't feel compelled to reach out to me
You're not in love, nor do you love me enough to keep it real with
me
I wanted to believe you'd love me right
So I held on to what I thought was right
But loving a man who doesn't really love me ain't fair
Passing time just to hear him tell me he does ain't right either
But it's what I wanted to hear
So why continue when I know he's not sincere?
Especially when there's another man who'd love to be where he is?
I know everything's for the moment, your buying time slowly,
As the clock winds down so do you only because I'm the one who
held us together
I wasn't ready or willing to give up on us, but believing in lying
words does not profit
I know I need to stop avoiding the inevitable, knock it and dissolve it
But why do good girls like bad boys
I've often wondered but now that I'm hooked I must acknowledge
It's one of those things that can't be explained
It's something I could never rationalize nor make any sense of
I want to be free, unable to love him, leave him be and move on

with ease

But all I ever wanted was for him to love me please, and only me

I know everything's for the moment you're buying time slowly as the clock winds down so do you only

Because I'm the one who held us together, if I ever stopped it would be the end of us

But wait,

Times up, I'm tired, exhausted, and your time has expired!

A Time

Once upon a time before you, before love, before the urgency
existed in me to love you
I was afraid to love, afraid to let anyone touch my heart,
I was emotionally untouchable,
Numb to all possibilities of what love could be
I had a closed heart and mind
Then you came along and moved me, enticed me, and slowly
ushered me into a place that forced me to reach for love and dared
me to fall in love
Once upon a time, once upon a time I had no one to confide in
There was no one I trusted enough to share my feelings with
No one worthy to let into my world
I was too personal to have my life showcased
I had too much pride to let anyone see my vulnerabilities and then
you came
You came so suddenly and showed me it was all right to trust---that
you could be trusted
You eased my heart and soothed my senses
You were my comfort, you did not judge me but you respected me
and
Embraced my vulnerabilities, loved me harder without taking any
thing away from my strengths
Once upon a time I was adamant about love and all it represented
I am no longer afraid,
You are my once upon a time in my life, when love is welcome...
Free, exuberating, and refreshing.

You are love.

My life wrapped up in the ups and downs of indifference. You are my forever love once upon a time NOW.

Declaration

Although we've had some hard times
It hasn't been too hard for me to throw up my hands and run
Run away from my feelings, run away from the facts, run away
from the truth, run away from reality, knowing that I'm loving you
all the more
I tell you, it seems the more we conquer one mountain,
It's another uphill battle of frustration and confusion, unanswered
questions and rumors
Surely this is a trial of love and consequences
I find myself feeling like everything is at stake
I want you to stay; I want us to remain one,
I want us to continue to grow
I need you to know, no matter
What things may seem like, look like, or feel like at times
I still love you all the more
It seems as if the more we collide the more my love abides
I can't begin to tell you how much you mean to me
I maintain because of the probability of your potential, time, and
the endurance of love and longevity,
I maintain because of hope and anticipation
The anticipation of one day fulfilling a void missing in our lives for
as long as I can remember
I remain faithful because you need a woman committed to you
regardless
Someone who loves you beyond mere words
Someone honest with you at all times,

Someone who believes in you when others doubt,
Someone who will be there when others fail you
Someone who will look past your faults and continue to love you in
spite of,
someone who will never let you fall
someone who will make you proud and esteem you when life is not
what it should be
I can't say I started loving you overnight
It was a process
It wasn't because of your looks, the way you walk or talk,
It was the potential I discerned from you
It was your passion for life and what it should be
It was your desire to right a wrong left unresolved in your life
It was the fact we have something in common, perhaps more than I
ever wanted to acknowledge,
Now regardless of what we go through, please know I may not be
all you ever dreamed of or imagined
I'm more than that and more so to become
This is my declaration of love and commitment to you for as long as
God allows.

What?

You say you've always prayed for a woman like me,
I remember that day oh so well
You had your moment to reminiscence on past loves-
The mistakes, heartbreaks, and unanswered questions
And still you claimed to have always wanted a woman like me
You said if you had a woman like me, you'd know what to do
As I reflect on how we connected, on how we first began,
I would have believed everything you ever stated
But because I was torn between my mind and my heart
I still questioned your sincerity,
Somewhere I internalized something you said,
      "you'd fear ever hurting me"
I held on to that like a parent promising to protect his child
You know I actually thought you meant what you said
As time went on we talked about men and women not persevering
in relationships, not being faithful to one another, not loving one
another as they should,
For some strange reason I thought you and I were on the same page.
I thought we would define love, commitment, and faithfulness, put
a new twist on trust, because of how we got down
I knew we would have obstacles,
And was prepared so I thought
However, I never thought you saying you loved me meant me and
several other women
I never thought that your idea of obstacles and tests consisted of
you disrespecting me, putting my feelings aside to fulfill your own

lustful desires,
I suppose I was too naïve.
After all I just didn't think about it
I remember us talking and you asking so casually if I thought I
wouldn't be tested like the women before me
I acknowledged that but never did I think in a million years
You would run game---in series to test my heart.
Never did I think you would openly engage in a relationship,
disregard my feelings or presence,
I set you at a much higher standard than that,
I thought we agreed no games, sideshows, or escapades?
I thought you cherished me? I thought you understood the whole
meaning of love?
I couldn't have been more wrong about you.
For some obscure reason, I thought you would appreciate me
I thought, I thought that's right I saw something different in you
Nevertheless, I was wrong.
Although I'm strong doesn't mean I don't feel
Because I'm understanding doesn't mean I should just be,
The fact that I proclaim to love you doesn't mean it ought not to be
reciprocated
As far as tests are concerned,
You've been tested as well
Now just so you know, although I haven't kicked up my heels
and pitched a fit over a woman you have chosen to keep ties with
doesn't mean I don't care or that I'm condoning what you're doing
Oh no by no means am I doing that
I am a strong believer you will reap what you have sown.

After all to her I may be the other woman, let the record speak for itself.

It was you and she before there ever was an us.

I suppose you failed to tell me that too?

Sometimes I look at you as if I don't know you,

Sometimes I look at you as if to say, you really think I'm stupid?

You asked me to give you time, to be patient with you

I granted your request knowing this here situation would ripen in just a matter of time.

I am faithful because that's all I know to be

This is how I was bred, but I sure 'nuff wasn't bred to be pissed on and stomped over.

I said I would not dissolve this relationship;

I'll give that pleasure to you, since it's been your pleasure principle all along.

It's not about me being insecure, it's about what's right

IF you can't be faithful over something little,

You sure wouldn't be faithful over much,

You were so caught up in you

You never gave me a second thought

As a matter of fact, what you *thought* you felt some time ago, left weeks before

Love is not just spoken words

Love is not just feelings,

Love is much deeper than that.

You said to speak upon anything like love now, would not be reality

Now, I couldn't agree more.

Yet you always wanted a woman like me, and now what?

You had a woman like me, but I still wasn't enough, and the love you *thought* you wanted you had…

The love you felt you needed, you had…

The woman you just had to have, you lost and now what?

Reconciliation

You were mind over matter,
You were laughter even when pain intensified,
You were tears when joy seemed impossible
You were the half I only thought existed in the confines of my own
mind
Someone who existed because of what I thought inside
You were the smile I often hid behind
You were contentment when I felt undefined
You were apart of me in so many ways
You understood me in ways that I needed not to explain
You and I were so much alike in so many ways that perhaps I just
forgot to give you what you needed
Perhaps I never really analyzed the differences among us for sake of
wanting to see what I wanted and needed from you
I always considered your needs but never fully processed them
accordingly as to exploit them so that you knew that I knew what
you needed of me.
I know you loved me---more than I thought.
Somehow I doubt if you knew how I truly loved you and rightfully
so...
I never gave you assurance, never gave you what you needed,
Although I was everything you wanted.
Our similarities existed in as much as our differences,
You were trying to find your way in life, longed for stability and
some financial return for all your years of schooling and hard work,
I just got sidetracked by your high maintenance life style and forgot

you were trying to make it just like I had some years before you.
Before I ever had thoughts of someone like you
You needed me and had I had your best interest at heart I would
have known that---
The fact I know now doesn't replace what you went through
It only brings one question to the forefront and that is---
Is your love strong enough to enable us to work out what went
wrong?
Or has your experience caused you so much pain that you can't
move beyond it?
Since I am what you wanted let me at least be the one you need
too?

Untitled

When I look at you, what do I see?
I see a man who's reluctant to expose his soul
Who's hesitant in expressing his emotions?
I see a man, who desires to be loved beyond a level of his own understanding,
I see a man who's captive to the political propaganda set to keep all black men bound and shackled.
I see a man, who wishes to be read from the mere look in his eyes,
I see a man who has had the finest women deemed fly by men
I see a man who desires a woman who will love him for all of his being
Not adding, substituting, or subtracting from his created ability to be,
I see a man who looks upon me as a woman with every quality conceivable to man
I indeed see a man, who's wavering in his spirit, between the shell and core of the woman he feels is destined for him
I see a man's who's wounded, frustrated, stagnated, and hurt by his current conditions.
I look at him,
I want him to internalize the fact that his situation is only a temporary state of being
That this here situation is only a trial of his faith,
I look at him and I want to soothe, caress, and ease his state of insecurity, doubts, and frustration
I need to mend his wounded heart

I want to eliminate all hurt and pain put upon him in this life of
social and economic disparity, and straight up political propagandaI
look at him I want to make everything, all things wrong in his
sight, right
I'll never give up on him,
I believe this man is destined for greatness
When I look at him,
I see a man who compliments my statue and being
I see a man who desires not to inflict any pain or hurt on me
But the greatest pain
The greatest hurt will come when he's not able to tell the truth than
To hold him high beneath his weakness in truth
I see a man whose very essence for being is power, prestige, and
privilege not the American Dream, but the HOPE and destiny of
all men destined for greatness.

Deception

You smile and talk sweetly, always you,
You seem to go out your way to show me, always me
That you'd do just about anything for me
To please me, make me happy, but why me?
Always you, so sudden and subtle but to look at you,
You seem to love me, but
I get this feeling deep down within
My inner being, my soul is not impressed inside,
Because my eyes and my heart can't seem to be vibe,
I'm baffle, what you say has me see you,
Always you, as if I don't know you
You look at me like you love me, always me and
Always you say you love me and only me
You say you do and do do me as if you do, but
I get this feeling deep down within my inner being,
My soul is not impressed inside
Because my eyes and my heart can't seem to vibe,
So sudden and subtle, you handled me haphazardly,
And I see, that you be, what you always be to only me, always me,
That one who says and does the opposite of what he claims to be,
With mine eyes the pictures not clear but with mine heart it tells
the story untold.

Heart Never Lies

The heart never lies, it tells the truth when words are unable to
convey the very essence of a situation,
The heart never lies, it teaches us when to trust and when to shield
ourselves from the painful encounters, which may seem unavoidable
to the naked eye,
The heart never lies, it conjugates and defines things we do and say,
Works as a detector to put time sensitive situations into perspective,
The heart never lies; it speaks at the most unexpected times and
forces one to acknowledge what lies ahead,
The heart never lies, it's a sensor for one's emotions, it enables one
to feel, sense, and extract from intuitions and experiences,
The heart never lies, it's a magnet for love, and it's a journey
through the emotions of pleasure and pain,
It's a force, which can stand alone, separate and apart from the mind
The heart never lies, it can disguise itself in crucial moments
detrimental to the mind, but it never lies,
It may induce pain, ache the very state of your being, but again, it
never lies
The mind may play tricks on you, but the heart is always true
That's why it conflicts with the mind at times;
The mind is rational and logical
The heart is sensitive to the emotions and omniscient to what you
feel
The heart ignites passion and warmth, hatred and fear
While the mind clearly delegates things in a sequence of black and
white, right and wrong

The heart promotes those grey areas of irrational segments of one's
life as to why one may love another or hate another,
The heart never lies,
It's unscripted and never premeditated
It's the way of the emotions
It's the sense of the feel,
It's graceful in nature with undesignated appeal,
The heart is forever changing, forever maturing, forever learning,
forever healing, and forever speaking as it evolves with time and
ignites the very essence of one's being.
I remind you…the heart never lies.

My Heart to Yours

If you could see my face whenever you call,
If you could hear my thoughts afar off,
If you could feel my heart when I think of you,
Then perhaps you'd understand how deep this is coming from-
My heart to yours.
If I could make up for all the bad relationships you've had,
If I could erase all your past hurts and ignite joy throughout your
spirit-I would.
If I could let you taste love on a whole new level-
I would.
If I could show you that love like this doesn't come everyday
Then you would know love-
From my heart to yours.
From my heart to yours,
I would show you the realities of what it means to love strong, hard,
and long
I would show you the effervescence of loving to agree and disagree--
--all in the same.
Simply a matter of love and respect
From my heart to yours.
The extremities of our non-verbal accolades is what defines our basis
for being who we are,
At the most unexpected times,
I know what you need to hear and feel,
I know what eases you at times when it seems nothing is going
quite right outside of the emotions we share,

I think of you and reflect on a reality that simplifies a lot of life's matters and issues for both you and I,
Love has always been a complex non-existent factor for me, but truth is you infuse the joy in love,
You extract love in me and disrupt intense sensational emotions that overwhelm the senses.
You're alluring and contagious, if there was ever any one thing I'd ever want you to know
It would be a matter of sequestering my love from my heart to yours.

Hope

Today is not like yesterday, and yesterday is a reminder of the other
day, but who's to say,
That your tomorrow will enable you to let go of what was
And strive for what may be and is subject to becoming your future
ambitions...
You're in a holding stance,
Only your mind can take you to tomorrow
Only your mind can cause you to dream a dream of freedom
A life of hope and promise
But right now, what you have to hold on to is hope

For every struggle, trial, and for every closed door,
Lies a new beginning
Closed doors only lead to new windows of opportunities,
Your past does not determine your end from your beginning
Every strike and every blemish creates a new pattern in life
So although you may not see what your tomorrow may be,
And although your obstacles may seem impossible to overcome,
Take refuge in the fact that nothing stays the same, and
Your situation and circumstances are subject to change.
So think and proclaim tomorrow
Being much better than your yesterday, and
Hope to change the sediments that once held you bound,
Set your heights on a new tomorrow full of expectation and
remember yesterday as just that a day that once was and is no longer.

53

Thank YOU

For each breath I take,
Knowing that without You I could not exist-
Thank You,
For every time I speak a word or hear a sound-
While it may seem simple, it's You who allows me to enjoy the
wonders of Your work, so-
I thank You,
For the times You allow me to feel, sense, and see-
To express emotions and describe all that You are-
I say thank You,
For the ability to reason, utilizing my cognitive skills is nothing to
take lightly, and for that-
I thank You
You gave me use of my faculty and limbs,
Beautified me, molded and made me into Your image, that's
nothing short of Your glory,
Therefore, for that I thank You-
My life should be a reflection of You, that's why
I mirror my life after You,
I forgive because You forgave me,
I believe because it's embedded in me,
From the womb, You knew me-
And through all my wounds, You healed me-
You are my Father, my beginning and end,
My protector and provider,
You are the man no other man can touch,

You see, You have been to me what no man has ever been and that
is faithful,
You are faithful even when I fall short,
You are consistent when all men falter,
You have dried every tear,
Chastised me when rebuke was needed, yet Your hand gentle and
meek,
You have imparted wisdom and knowledge; please don't let me
forget discernment-
You have graciously given me the ability to recognize deceit-
You are my covering, my safe haven, my refuge, and there is
nothing You can't do-
You keep proving Yourself repeatedly,
I need You and will always need You,
You never needed me, yet You still choose to use me even when I
am least deserving of Your time and attention-
I don't just need You,
I want to serve You,
I am nothing without You,
My life would be empty and meaningless,
I think and when I ponder thoughts of You,
I just can't thank You enough!
I thank You not for all that you do, but for who You are-
You alone are worthy of much more than thanks so I strive to live a
life that is pleasing in Your Sight!